Super7 Operations

The Next Step for Lean in Financial Services

Menno R. van Dijk, MSc

iUniverse LLC
Bloomington

SUPER7 OPERATIONS
THE NEXT STEP FOR LEAN IN FINANCIAL SERVICES

iUniverse books may be ordered through booksellers or by contacting:

iUniverse
1663 Liberty Drive
Bloomington, IN 47403
www.iuniverse.com
1-800-Authors (1-800-288-4677)

ISBN: 978-1-4917-1350-1 (sc)
ISBN: 978-1-4917-1352-5 (hc)
ISBN: 978-1-4917-1351-8 (e)

Library of Congress Control Number: 2013921910

Printed in the United States of America.

iUniverse rev. date: 11/27/2013

FOREWORD

This is a book about impactful change. There are many theories on operational excellence, but few deliver on their promise. Our people do their best to keep their promise every day by delivering great service to our customers, working closely together, and showing the flexibility to adapt to ever-changing customer demands.

ING aims to build the preferred bank: the bank you love to do business with. At the time we developed that objective, we focused on earning our customers' trust through transparent products, value for money, and superior service. For daily banking business, this translated to delivering exactly the service that the customer wants, when and where he or she wants it. In operations, we had started to measure process performance some years earlier. Our organisation quickly needed to become more customer centred, and many initiatives were started to improve on end-to-end process performance.

We captured our ideas on what a good process should look like in a set of ten principles, to which every ING customer operational process had to adhere. An example of this is that many of our paper forms are rapidly being replaced by digital dialogues that make use of all information that we already have. This way, a customer never needs to fill in the same information twice.

During this time, Super7 Operations was developed within Operational Services in Leeuwarden, our centralised operations department that handles most of the day-to-day customer requests. The results were impressive. Just as IT changes are sped up and made 'agile' by putting people together in scrum teams, Super7 Operations cuts throughput times to one day (Today In, Today Out [TITO]), and our organisation is flexible enough to adopt to all fluctuations in daily demand. To underline the innovative nature of this change: Super7 Operations at ING was nominated for the 2012 Dutch NCCA award for innovation.

For me, this book celebrates the dedication and hard work of all the people at ING Operational Services and ING Business Change that were involved in creating the success of Super7 Operations. I hope you will enjoy reading it.

—Bart Schlatmann
Chief Operating Officer (COO)
ING Domestic Bank
The Netherlands

CONTENTS

INTRODUCTION

I have been always amazed by what is achieved when a production team, with operators and maintenance engineers working closely together, improves their own production line step by step. I've seen this many times throughout my fifteen years of working as a lean consultant (as of this writing). The first signs of improvement appear after the team gets training and starts applying the principles of lean. The team finds the first quick wins, and this immediately creates enthusiasm and momentum. The real transformation happens, however, when the team begins to truly cooperate. They become an improvement team, committed to improve performance, making optimal use of the strengths of each of the team members. When they really get going and continuous improvement starts, it's just wonderful to witness.

Printing lines double their weekly output within one year, with their set-up times reduced from two and a half hours to twenty minutes. The filthiest printing ink-fill lines turn into spotlessly clean and well-organised production lines. And, most of all, production workers rediscover the fun in their work and regain a sense of pride in the performance of their production line.

I've been working as a lean and Lean Six Sigma consultant since 1998. Over the years, I've introduced the concept of improvement teams within a dozen production companies within the Netherlands, and a few in Germany. In these multidisciplinary teams, people from different departments work together on the single task of improving a production line, making it run faster and smoother, reducing downtime and breakdowns, etc. Individuals that are part of a team have the flexibility to cope with any production problem that can occur. For me, the people on the shop floor aren't 'resources' that need to be 'managed', but, rather, creative and knowledgeable individuals who can do great things, especially when they truly work together.

Later in my career, I was asked to introduce lean in other types of organisations: logistics, retail, healthcare, and financial services. I've always enjoyed these kinds of projects: translating what I had learned in production to a completely different setting, applying the same underlying principles, and making them work in practice. In my most recent position as an internal consultant at ING Bank, I implemented these ideas in what I, and others, feel is an innovative way – Super7 Operations.

Lean itself has been around in financial services for over ten years (as of this writing). However, among the insurance companies and banking back offices that I saw, the implementation of lean in this context usually focuses on making the operation manageable and controllable. This was generally accomplished by introducing standard processing times and reports on productivity and availability, and also by making the performance visual on the shop floor. (Throughout this book, 'shop floor' refers to the forum where employees handle customer requests or interact directly with customers.)

In my view, these back offices consistently lacked a key element of lean: the *fun* factor – the experiments, the improvements, the supportive management style, and the teamwork. Moreover, I didn't see the sense of invigoration and renewal that comes when employees on the shop floor experience the improvements brought on by a lean implementation.

And, perhaps even more importantly, the 'old' lean that I encountered in financial services failed to put the *customer* in the centre. Instead, these approaches focused mainly on cost containment and internal service level agreements (SLAs).

To my mind, this approach to lean sidesteps its most essential benefits and its central point. From what I saw, lean within financial services needed a new go. In response, I developed a new approach – *Super7 Operations* – which we will discuss in this book.

Discovering the True Benefits of Lean

The true benefits of Lean

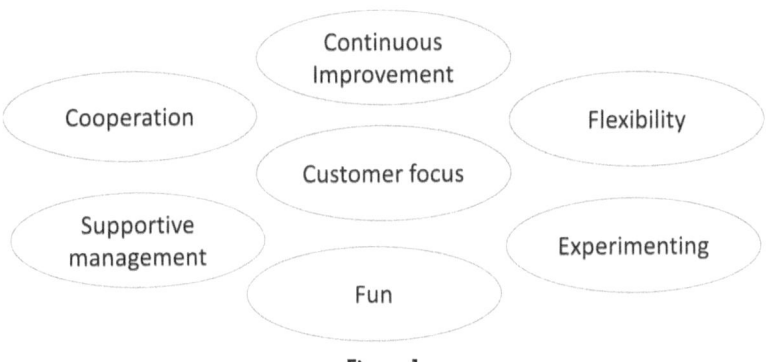

Figure 1

What I've concluded from all of my projects (over fifty now) is that the true power of lean and Lean Six Sigma lies with this concept – getting the customer into the hearts and minds of the people of the shop floor and their managers, and getting them to truly work together to achieve continuous improvement. Sure, a one-time improvement designed by a specialist (Six Sigma Black Belt or Green Belt) or production technician can yield a significant improvement of the productivity of a production team. In my experience, however, the momentum often fades over time. One year after, you should be happy if the initial gain has been retained; however, when a production team really commits to improving their own work, and understands the value of their work for the customer, you shouldn't be surprised to see 20 or even 50 per cent improvement, one year after the start of the programme.

And the next year. *And the next.*

Another thing I've learned is that management plays a crucial role in this cooperation and continuous improvement. 'A self-steering team needs a lot of steering,' one of my lean teachers once told me – this may have been said in jest, but there is an element of truth in it. Effective lean management means continuously improving the work and stimulating the production teams to do the same.

A lean manager asks a team to deliver on output (perfect quality products), but also to start an improvement cycle each time a problem, defect, or other non-quality issue occurs. A lean manager is present on the shop floor, accessible for the people, and available for support and escalation whenever needed. Should the team be unable to fix the problem themselves, their manager is there to help. And if the individual manager can't help, it may be necessary to ask for help from other teams or from the manager's manager; if needed, the research and development (R&D) department steps in to redesign, or the plant manager gets involved. The whole management pyramid is upside down, supporting the production teams in doing their jobs and improving the entire process.

Now let's get back to the *fun* aspect of lean. In my work, I always love to experiment. Start pilots, test out new ways of working. This has helped me greatly in all of my projects. And when I get the shop floor teams themselves to start experimenting, that's the moment that I'm almost certain that the project will be a success. There's fun and excitement in watching a printing line being set on a slightly faster pace, waiting to find out what mishap will occur (breaking paper, splashing ink, etc.), and then discovering that nothing goes wrong; after which it starts all over again, increasing the pace until the team does find something they can start improving on. Or, imagine a back office, where the same type of paper form has been typed over and over again into the administration system by the same people for years and years. Now imagine what would happen if you implemented a pilot, where you put together people of different departments in a small multidisciplinary team, working without inventory and without batches. It's exciting to see the extent of streamlining that can result just from creating that team, which we call a Super7 [see Chapter 1 for full definition].

For me, that kind of effective streamlining is the most fun you can have in any back office – and the same applies to the participants on the shop floor as well, in my experience. The Super7 principle is the result of some exciting experimentation, which we will explore together throughout this book.

Section 1 of this book focuses on real-world practices in the financial sector. Managers and employees working in financial services might get some valuable ideas for improving customer service in their own back offices, instead of waiting for the long-promised 'straight through processing' IT changes to deliver. The rest of Section 1 provides a solid foundation from which to build a Super7 Operations System within your own organisation.

As for the make-up of the rest of this book, the case studies in Section 2 may be of use for anyone who is interested in lean operations – consultants, practitioners, and teachers alike, allowing them to see what is possible with lean after operational management. Section 3, on the other hand, looks at other situations where Super7 could be useful (i.e., outside of the financial sector).

Whatever your intended purpose in reading this book might be, I hope that it will inspire you to experiment and explore, to come up with your own innovative ways to incorporate the concepts of Super7 into your own work environment.

SECTION 1

Super7 Operations

I n this section of the book, we will examine the dynamics of implementing Super7 within the operations of an organisation – specifically, within the financial services sector. Replacing older lean techniques with Super7 can, and does, transform organisations. This section will explain the ways to effectively streamline the process of optimising the back-office system in a financial organisation.

CHAPTER 1

Super7 – The Logical Next Step for Lean within Financial Services

A few years ago I was given the opportunity to complete a significant task – optimising the back office at the Leeuwarden branch of a Dutch bank called ING. What began as an experiment in implementing lean in this back office eventually developed into something else: a new solution, and one with the potential to redefine lean and its application within the financial services industry. We call this solution *Super7*.

Super7 Defined

Super7 Operations are based on the principle of dividing traditional-size teams into small teams of five to nine persons. Each small team is called a Super7, and every Super7 receives a fixed percentage of the work of the larger group.

Each Super7 team has the task of completely finishing all of their customer requests from start to finish, directly the same day, without making the customer wait. In most cases, implementing Super7 Operations makes it possible to work without inventory and without handovers. This means that a complex workflow-management or inventory-management system is no longer necessary.

3

The small Super7 team creates flexibility in skills: if a customer request requires several different tasks, a multi-skilled Super7 is created that can finish all tasks within the team. The team size is effective, and because the teams are small, they allow for visibility and trust, which in turn enables the team to make effective decisions. It's almost impossible for a traditional team of twenty to twenty-five persons to make a decision that everybody is happy about.

Finally, every Super7 has control over how they do the work: who does what, in what order, and at what pace – all are the responsibility of the Super7. Super7s are steered only on output, on what they deliver. And they can ask their managers for help at any time. The Super7 applies the principles of lean and operational management, with autonomy and responsibility on the shop floor.

The most recent trend in this space, operational management, has achieved some impressive results, causing a true lean-hype at banks since the early 2000s. What I have found in my own experience in the last few years, however, is that it's now time for the next step beyond operational management, via the kind of new approach offered by Super7.

The Limitations of Operational Management in Back Offices

Lean was first introduced in the world of banking via the back office, as this environment was the bank department most similar to the production environment (i.e., shop floor) where lean originated – the manufacturing and assembly plants of Toyota. The lean basics [*see* figure 1] and well-known lean best practices [*see* figure 2] like standardised work, takt (pace of manufacturing time [from the German]) and standardised cycle times, visual management, and production levelling were all translated into a system for the bank back office. This system is what we call *operational management,* and it consists of the following:

4

- standard times for each type of customer requests
- work packages of exactly one hour of work each, assigned to individual employees on an hourly basis
- work held in inventory with planned production to level out peaks and lows in customer demands
- performance measurement, which measure and direct employee availability and productivity, with matching target setting on all levels in the organisation
- team boards visualising team performance versus targets; weekly meetings with the team
- regular continuous improvement sessions on the shop floor

Leeuwarden had adopted operational management a few years prior to my arrival, and at the time, everybody was very enthusiastic about it. When I arrived at Leeuwarden, however, the initial sheen was off the rose, so to speak. Operational management was not having the desired effect anymore. In fact, the performance of their back office had ING entirely puzzled.

Despite the implementation of lean, customer goodwill was at an all-time low, with production lagging consistently behind customer requests. With all the lean best practices in place, why were the customers complaining so much about the service they received? And, when operational management had always been the most effective solution for meeting customer expectations, why was the organisation now unable to meet those expectations when applying that solution to the situation?

Simply put, the old methods weren't cutting it within the evolving world of financial services. The way we used to do operational management wasn't enough for what banking was becoming.

The integration of Web-based services into the customer experience of businesses across a wide array of sectors had changed the time frame of customers' perception of what quality customer service is. Via the Internet, customers had become accustomed to a new level of service; for instance, a Web-hosting contract is closed within minutes, with digital forms, e-mail confirmations, and all the necessities provided online.

The customer question became: why do I have to wait more than a week for my bank to answer a simple request/question? Perhaps even more importantly, as a result of the global financial crisis, customer trust was at an all-time low. We needed a new approach in place that could increase efficiency on the shop floor and directly address customer needs, assuaging both the rise in customer expectations and the rise in customer complaints.

Super7 — Rethinking the Back Office

Super7 Operations, as described in this book, provided the new approach that answered the prevailing dilemma at ING. And what worked for ING, perhaps, could work for more financial-sector back offices searching for the next lean breakthrough, the next logical step after operational management, and the one that would transform the financial sector's processes, culture, and customer relationships.

Clearly, the lean trend within financial services is far from over. According to recent research[1], banks and other financial institutions that have successfully implemented lean programmes record 15 per cent to 25 per cent improvement in overall efficiency. Although the banking crisis forced banks to rethink their business, their proposition, and their priorities, lean (with its core elements of continuous improvement, waste reduction, process thinking, and customer-centricity) is still an important pillar in the strategy of a large number of leading banks.

Super7 builds off these core principles and successful applications of lean within the financial space in a new and promising way. Moreover, in the wake of operational management, there clearly is a need for the next lean programme that can transform the space. Super7 has proved to be just that. It is not a departure from lean but a dynamic enhancement. Simply stated, Super7 is the sought-after next logical step.

In the subsequent chapters within this section, we will explore just how Super7 works, describing its attributes and benefits, examining some examples of how it manifests in the back office, and seeing the results it can produce.

The Basic Steps of Lean

1. Focus on customer value: what is the value that the end-customer is willing to pay for?
2. Map the value stream: what are the steps that we take to get this value to the customer?
3. Learn to recognise waste: inventory, defects, overproduction, waiting, transport (products), motion (people), overprocessing. Waste is anything that doesn't add value for the customer.
4. Eliminate as much waste as possible.
5. Create flow in the value stream: continuous flow instead of batch-and-queue production.
6. Let the customer pull the value through the value stream: production is started by customer demand, and demand is translated from the customer backwards through the value stream.
7. Improve continuously; always look for new ways to work with even less waste, with the help of the extensive lean toolbox.

Based on the (highly recommended) book: *Lean Thinking* by Womack & Jones[2]

CHAPTER 2

The Development of Super7 at ING

In 2011, I dug into my new project at ING – helping to improve the back office of Operational Services (OS) in Leeuwarden. Customer service was in need of improvement, with customer requests taking days or sometimes weeks to process, leaving many customers wondering if they would ever receive a proper answer to their requests. I was tasked with streamlining the back office and increasing throughput in order to (1) get customer needs addressed in a timely manner, and (2) get customer loyalty and satisfaction back in a safe zone for the organisation.

When I arrived in Leeuwarden, they had already had lean in place for a few years. Employees were responsible for their own hour packages. All the work was sorted into customer requests of the same type, and each type of work was given a standard completion time. In this way, every employee had a standard amount of time to work on each customer request. Managers gathered the incoming requests, preparing them and then saving them up for processing the next day by individual employees. When that work was meted out to individual employees the next day, they each were tasked with addressing exactly the number of hour packages to satisfy the eight-hour workday.

Despite this seemingly accurate way of matching work to capacity, it required a lot of management attention to ensure that all work packages had been completed at the end of the day. If an hour package was not completed in a workday, it was sent back into production planning and work distribution for readdressing the next day.

The employees were productive and committed to the set goal, but their commitment to that goal was based on the SLA, not the actual customer. Their efficiency didn't answer an obligation to what ostensibly was ING's main concern – the customer – but to an 'internal process owner' that addressed customer needs as 'inventory'.

The old process

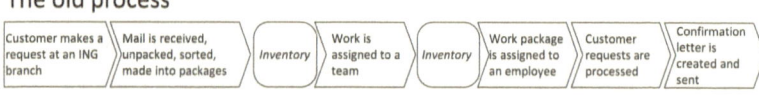

Figure 2

It wasn't 'inventory' by any stretch of the imagination. After all, where was the benefit to the customer? Think of it this way: if you go to a store to buy a jar of peanut butter, having that inventory stocked on the shelf benefits you as a customer. But that paradigm cannot apply within a bank. It was not as if one of ING's employees could respond to an address change, say, with something they already had on the shelf. 'Here, take this address change I already had prepared beforehand…'; naturally, that wouldn't do the job. What we essentially had on our hands was not inventory but *backlog*.

The Problem

The dilemma with this backlog was that, simply put, work was lying around. One day before the end of an SLA, the inventory management system would prioritise inventory as 'orange'; on the last day or beyond, it would mark it as 'red'. By and large, this system of prioritisation meant that work would sit around waiting to become orange.

When tasks were finally parcelled to an employee for processing, that employee would inevitably be under pressure to finish because of the standard times. If anything about the task was unclear, if any bit of critical information was missing, the employee would just 'reject' the task and send it back to the customer.

It wasn't difficult to understand why this process was leaving customers disgruntled and ready to jump ship. Take a moment to imagine this process from the customer's end. A customer has submitted a request and has patiently waited for a response, only to ultimately receive a note that the form was rejected. Not the best way to foment customer satisfaction, or customer loyalty, for that matter. In fact, at the time, the 'processes' (customer requests) handled at the Leeuwarden back office had a Net Promoter Score (NPS) in the range of –30, so customer loyalty was thin on the ground, to say the least. Clearly, customers held a lot of resentment about how the team at Leeuwarden processed customer requests.

Naturally, the ING organisation had already started many initiatives to improve its customer-service procedures. For example, instead of sending rejected forms back to the customer, ING would first try to contact the customer to explain what went wrong and what information was missing; if possible, the back office would try to correct the problem directly. Customers appreciated the improved level of service. Naturally, all successful initiatives were incorporated into our solution.

The Solution — Developing Super7 Operations

I saw the situation at Leeuwarden as an opportunity to develop a new approach to lean within a bank setting. The challenge before me was increasing throughput and eradicating the backlog. I also needed to reprioritise employee productivity and focus, and make sure that the end goal satisfied customer needs.

It seemed to me that the first order of business was to eliminate any inventory older than one day. It made sense to me to start working a system of Today In, Today Out (TITO).

The problem was that work preparation typically took about 75 per cent of the day, leaving only 25 per cent of the day to actually process the tasks. It occurred to me that instead of dividing the work up among individuals, we might divide the work up among small groups. How small? Groups of seven, with each group comprised of team members that united all the necessary skills to accomplish tasks in one day. That's how the core idea of Super7 was born.

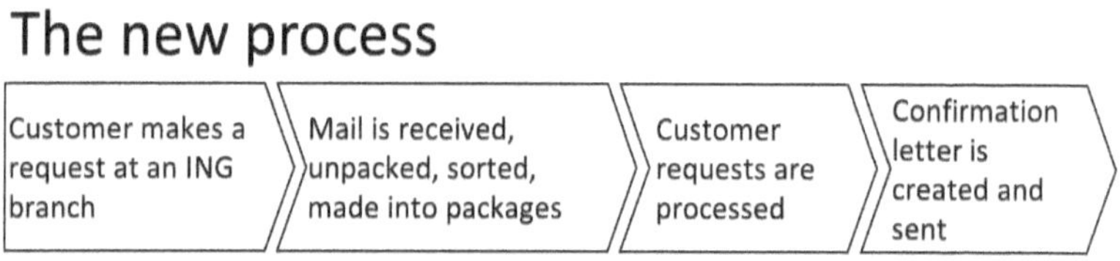

The new process

| Customer makes a request at an ING branch | Mail is received, unpacked, sorted, made into packages | Customer requests are processed | Confirmation letter is created and sent |

Figure 3

Before the development of Super7, the back office continually addressed work from a few days before. The logistics department would receive the forms and begin preparing the work into work streams and hour packages. Management would then sit in on a daily production meeting in order to determine who was going to undertake which work the *next* day – already a day behind. Best case scenario, an employee was *at the earliest* doing the work of yesterday, and, more often than not, work that was much older than that.

In addition to implementing a team that could handle the workflow in a single day, I knew that we needed to seriously reduce the logistics involved. Since teams would now be in place, portioning tasks was redundant; in fact, the daily production meeting was eliminated entirely, with work instead sent to the same physical location on a daily basis.

This made the workday far more efficient. Logistics now took the first part of the morning (from 7 a.m. to 9 a.m.) to open and sort customer mail (i.e., tasks,) and partition these tasks into packages of the same type. A single package of a single type of task was then sent to a single Super7 team that would address that package in a single day.

Some work streams were too small to have seven people working on them. We developed a solution for this by creating multi-skilled Super7 teams.

Super7 – All-in-one

Figure 4

A single multi-skilled Super7 would work on all the requests of several types of requests, finishing the total volume of these requests the same day. There were also a couple of work streams that were too large for one Super7. These were assigned to two or three Super7s, each responsible for a fixed percentage of the daily volume.

Assigning all the work of the entire department to Super7s was quite a puzzle, as you can imagine. However, with logistics streamlined and tasks reprioritised, employee focus was now on customer requests, rather than feeding an internal machine and shuffling work back and forth. The focal shift was subtle, but nonetheless significant. The priority was once again the customer, and the bank could only be the better for it.

Super7 and the Ongoing Reduction of Waste

Reduction of the seven types of waste is a central point of the lean philosophy: inventory, overproduction, overprocessing, non-quality, motion (of people), transport (of the product), and waiting; plus, the three later added wastes: talent waste, material/environmental waste, and non-safety.

Waste is everywhere. Waste is a natural and unavoidable extension of production. In a world without waste, we wouldn't need to have any transport, waiting, inventory, etc., to get an automobile. You would simply make your wish known, and — *poof!* — your no-waste car would magically appear right next to you. That, of course, is just not going to happen. So is the quest against waste irrational?

From my perspective, when making improvements, focusing on reducing waste points you in the right direction. As long as you keep reducing waste, without creating more waste at another point in the process, you're moving in the right direction.

When I look at processes, I try to look at the process from the customer's perspective. Do we make the customer wait for the product? How much transport takes place in order to get the product from one department to the next before it's delivered to the customer? And, with every processing step, I ask myself: Does this add value — for the customer?

One time, I was talking to the manager of a life insurance back office. The process of opening an insurance policy was taking several days. A customer request went through three processing steps, each step taking one workday to finish. 'Why is that?' I asked the manager. 'It's like painting a door,' he said. 'After each layer, the paint must dry before you can put on the next layer. Our system runs nightly batches, so there's nothing we can do.'

All this waiting bugged me, however. Because it's not at all like painting doors; in fact, the freshly entered customer request doesn't need to dry. Waiting makes a paint job better, yes, but waiting doesn't make life insurance better. I made some calls to the system specialists: there were batches, but the first three steps could be processed in one single batch run. They didn't have to wait, they just assumed that they had to. A quick win was found.

Super7 and TITO are based on the principle that customer requests shouldn't ever lie around, waiting to be completed. A freshly received customer request doesn't have to dry, doesn't have to cool down, doesn't have to wait — waiting is waste. TITO reduced the wait time for picking up customer requests to less than one day, every day.

CHAPTER 3

Three Reasons to Introduce Super7 in Your Operation

In my experiences with the development and implementation of Super7, I have found that there are myriad benefits to a business – on both the micro and macro levels – when the organisation employs these techniques in a back office. The nature of these benefits can vary from sector to sector. Consistently, however, three central benefits come up again and again:

- customer-centric and employee-empowered business culture
- reduced inventory
- more supportive management style

We will look at each of the above central benefits in detail throughout this chapter, as they are the three essential reasons for implementing Super7 at an organisation. Together, these three form an enterprise-wide transformation, bringing new and enhanced value to everything from the point-of-contact with the customer to shop floor processes. As such, I have found Super7 to be one of the most comprehensive solutions for improving the performance and efficiency of an organisation.

The first – evolving a new customer-centric and employee-empowered business culture via Super7 – is possibly the most difficult to delineate. The concept of business culture itself has always been somewhat amoebic, involving factors that often function on an intuitive level rather than a factual one. What I have seen, however, is that Super7 realigns the *intent* behind workflow in a way that naturally and clearly redefines the culture of an organisation. By restructuring the way employees handle tasks, Super7 automatically switches employee focus onto the customer.

Old situation	Super7 Operations
Efficiency centricity • One-hour packages: the pace is monitored on an hourly basis • Individual productivity targets for all employees	Customer centricity • Super7 deliver service to the customer • They finish everything that the customer asks them that day • Targets are: work Today-In, Today Out (no inventory), in cooperation with your Super7
Limited contact between customers and operations • E-mails are received within the logistics department, then printed and processed like paper forms • No direct telephone contact with customers	Direct contact between customer and operations: • E-mails are received within the Super7, and are processed the same day • If there's anything missing on the customer's request, the Super7 calls the customer to fix the problem.
Employee is responsible for a part of the process	Super7 team is responsible for the entire process
Not much responsibility for the customer requests • Incomplete form? Reject, and on to the next form • Additional question? No time, so forward request to another team	High level of responsibility • Do what is needed to help the customer • Autonomy in determining who does what and how the work is done
Long throughput time, high inventory • Inventory and an inventory management system, with sometimes differences between the two • Steering on inventory, to keep the work load level at all times (but the customer has to wait when it's busy)	Today In, Today Out (received today, processed before 8 p.m.) • No inventory, no inventory management system, no inventory differences that need to be corrected • Quick response management during the day, to maintain Today In, Today Out (almost) every day.
Input management, tight control • Additional management layer, keeping track of the pace on an hourly basis • Maximizing the available time of the employees, with a tight control on productivity	Output management • The *how* is left to the Super7 • The manager is there during the day, to help with issues or problems
Large teams, with each member doing his or her own work.	Small teams, together responsible for a common task • Visibility, trust, open communication
No difference on the shop floor between a busy day and a quiet day	Team has an ambitious target and goes for it!

Old Situation versus Super7 Operations

We've isolated the three main benefits and reasons to implement Super7, now let's define them each a bit more.

Firstly, not only does this transform shop floor employees' attitudes towards their work, but it also consequently improves the experience of end users (i.e., customers). This in turn reduces incoming customer requests, streamlining the workload and increasing productivity. This benefits both workflow and customer satisfaction.

Secondly, Super7 brings an increased flexibility to the structure of the shop floor, allowing companies to deal easily with fluctuations in tasks and work requests. This second benefit and reason to implement Super7 is much more 'nuts and bolts' and easier to quantify than the first. Much like the kind of smaller, more specialised machines you might see on a lean assembly line, a Super7 shop floor uses individual, specific skills of each team member within the Super7 team to address certain tasks in the timeliest manner. Super7 also encourages shared learning between team members, building in contingency plans for handling certain tasks if a specialised employee is not on hand and thereby increasing the flexibility of the team as a whole.

Lastly, Super7 enables a more supportive managerial style. This third benefit/reason might seem ironic on some levels, since Super7 is actually designed to allow for more autonomy from the shop floor employees. From the management perspective, however, the manager is meant to move from micromanaging to a more results-oriented approach. In this way, a manager's engagement with the shop floor is more about adding value and less about controlling. This foments more positive interaction with management from the shop floor, which naturally leads to many associated benefits.

These three reasons for implementing Super7 form a wide-ranging and truly transformative approach to lean production, one that I see leading a new era of lean at financial institutions. Let's explore each reason individually and in greater detail.

Reason 1 — Customer-Focused and Employee-Empowered Culture
Realigning focus on the customer, and enhancing cooperation and teamwork

Better Quality through Optimal Use of Unique Abilities

There's a simple truth I think most of us can agree on: people work better when they work on something they are *good* at. We each have our own unique ability (or abilities), or a particular activity that we excel in, and Super7 takes advantage of this.

Under Super7, a team benefits when each person can make more use of his or her unique ability. When the person works on an activity using this unique ability, efficiency increases, and the average time taken to complete the activity also increases. As a result, the productivity of the entire team improves.

Team members under Super7 also work *together* to determine how they can enhance individual and team productivity by leveraging team member skills.

In a Super7, team members are proactive about identifying their strengths and which tasks they feel they are the best match for. Team members also make recommendations as to which tasks they feel would be the best match for another colleague. In biweekly sessions, the team reassigns and allocates work according to skill, maximising productivity by matching each team member to his or her ideal task.

Ownership of Customer Requests

The Super7 structure also redefines the nature of a task for an employee, giving each worker a healthy sense of ownership in each assignment. Instead of looking at tasks and thinking, 'This is my stack of work,' under Super7, an employee thinks, 'These are my customers for today.'

What are the results of that shift? At ING the implementation of Super7s showed an increased willingness on the part of employees to *take the extra steps* needed to successfully complete a task.

Yes, finishing their tasks quickly in order to get home on time were still motivators for employees, but something interesting happened. Previously, completing a work package left an employee beholden to the clock; whereas now, under Super7, completing a customer request made the employee beholden to the actual customer.

Is it time to go home yet?

Figure 5

Let's look at a specific example in order to illustrate this further.

Before Super7, a request to switch to a different type of checking account would come in via a filled-in form (paper). As an aside, the customer has written on it: 'By the way, I've moved. New address is Pivot Drive 10 in Haarlem, the Netherlands.' Before Super7, the employee, whose evaluation was then based on productivity, would see this note but ignore it. After all, the extra request would result in missing the one-hour deadline for the work package at hand. Best case scenario, the employee might have asked the 'water spider' (i.e.,

Menno R. van Dijk, MSc

work distributor) to take the request to someone who was doing address changes that day.

Under Super7, every employee's orientation is now on satisfying customer needs. The additional task at hand is a customer request and therefore part of the employee's key mission, not an annoying extra. Because the employee sees the addition on the form as 'a request from the customer', the employee finishes both requests. If unsure of how to accomplish this, the employee will ask within the Super7; most likely, a Super7 colleague does know. As a result, the customer becomes the first priority, and the employee handles the request in order to serve the customer.

Super7 Contributes to a Cooperative, Customer-Oriented Culture

The Super7 mindset

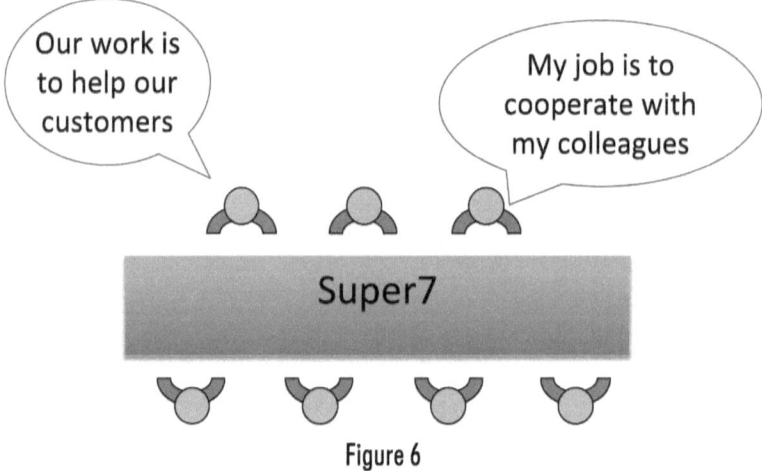

Figure 6

More-efficient processing of customer requests is a huge benefit, but there's an even more critical transition that takes place following the implementation of Super7. The culture of the organisation instantly and automatically reorients towards the customer.

On the micro level, small changes, such as changing a task

from a 'work package' to 'our customers' requests', initiates an important psychological shift for employees. The focus is no longer on a mechanical component, something that satisfies a machine; rather, the focus is on a person-to-person task. In other words, the employee's conception of a task goes from 'this must be done to meet a requirement' to 'completing this task helps someone'.

This new focus on the customer doesn't stop with employee perception of their own work. Rather, it colours their perception of the entire organisation's work, redefining the company from a system that demands work packages to an organisation focused on customer satisfaction.

The cooperative and collaborative nature of Super7 also signals a shift to employees. Employees no longer work alone, but as part of a collective. The positive effects of this collaborative structure flow in both directions: employees feel supported by the team while simultaneously feeling an enhanced sense of self-worth as a result of helping the team, which benefits the team, the organisation, and, ultimately, the customer.

Employees no longer feel like automatons set to work on redundant tasks day in and day out. They are now engaging in results-oriented activities that highlight their own usefulness and contain a human element that makes the work even more gratifying.

Perhaps even most importantly, customers notice the difference. In a case study of the after-effects of implementing Super7, customers were *clearly* impressed with the results. The organisation's NPS increased by 28 points, while customer satisfaction with throughput time skyrocketed 77 percentage points. Customers also noted that they had to initiate far fewer status calls to check in on their requests, signalling that their requests were addressed in a timelier manner. Perhaps this in turn fomented their confidence that their requests were competently handled. Timeliness leads customers to feel employees are efficient *and* effective.

So you see from this that an enhanced focus on the customer and a shift in culture from 'processes' to 'customer' makes for a much more productive organisation.

Optimal Team Size for Lean

What is the optimal team size for lean working? This question keeps popping up. In several recent publications on Scrum[3], an optimal team size of 7 plus or minus 2 (that's 5 to 9 to you and me) is mentioned. Stephen Robbins, author of *Essentials of Organizational Behavior*[4], a best-selling textbook on organisational behaviour, has concluded that teams of more than 10 to 12 people have a difficult time establishing feelings of trust, mutual accountability, and cohesiveness. Without these, constructive interaction is difficult. At the SPA 2009 conference[5], Joseph Pelrine told his audience that the sizes 5, 15, and 150 have been mentioned in (or can be derived from) scientific research, as being optimal sizes for social groups. To me, 150 sounds too big, not to mention impractical, for an autonomous team. Some people are convinced that a team should have an odd number of team members so that a democratic decision will always have a majority. In this respect, 8 is mentioned as the most problematic team size. And then there is the principle of social loafing, first demonstrated by psychologist Max Ringelmann in the 1910s when he measured the pressure exerted by individuals and teams pulling on a rope. Groups of 3 exerted only 2½ times (not 3 times) the average individual pressure. Groups of 8 exhibited less than 4 times the individual average. Ringelmann's and related studies have shown that individual effort is inversely related to team size. But is effort the same as effectiveness, especially when the work does not require physical labour, but, rather, intelligence and judgement? My analysis, based on all of these sources and my own experience in lean teams, results in the following graph:

Analysis of team effectiveness versus team size

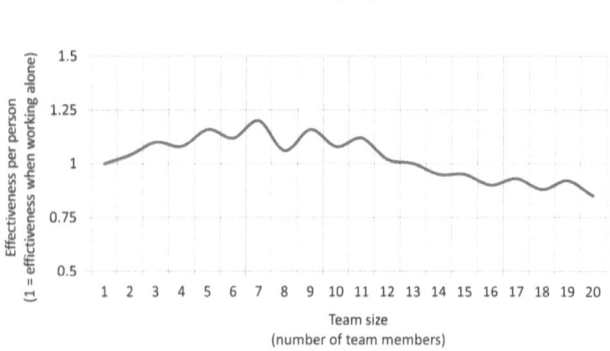

Figure 7

Reason 2 — Flexibility to Cope with Fluctuation
Because inventory costs way too much time and money

Super7 Uses Flexibility, Not Inventory, to Cope with Fluctuation

Fluctuation is an issue that can plague many organisations. The natural phenomenon of peaks and lows in the amount of customer requests can leave management and personnel unsure of how to address tasks in a timely and efficient manner. Level demand is much easier – and cheaper – and fluctuation makes production planning difficult.

In the past, queues (keeping customer requests in inventory) were used to level out demand. Toyota has taught the world that inventory equals waste. In fact, lean hates fluctuation so much, that lean gurus use the Japanese term for it: *mura*. (Just as they call waste *muda*.) Queuing cannot inherently be the lean solution.

There are three ways to cope with fluctuation:

1. Inventory (delivery from stock, or keeping customer orders in queue)
2. Overcapacity (planning the capacity to be able to cope with the peaks in demand)
3. Flexibility (letting capacity move with the tide of fluctuation)

What's at issue with inventory? Quite a lot. Lean specialists from all over the world have written extensively about the issues with inventory, so there are many responses to consider. It's a good question for framing this discussion, but let's keep the answers simple:

- For customers, inventory means waiting.
- For your company, inventory requires resources and management attention.

And what's wrong with overcapacity? After all, overcapacity isn't one of the seven types of Waste, according to the lean experts. This is true enough; however, it's costly. You always need a little bit of overcapacity, for working on improvements, kaizens, projects, etc., but there is an optimum balance to achieve. Too much of anything, even a good thing, is rarely the best practice.

The leanest way to cope with fluctuation is to make the resources flexible. For instance, lean companies prefer using several smaller, versatile machines with low set-up times over one large, specialised, high-capacity machine.

Lean back offices don't have large machines, and being more flexible automatically means that your personnel need to be more flexible. The first way to achieve flexibility is by using multi-skilled personnel instead of highly specialised personnel. A second way is to use flexible contract forms (e.g., contract for twenty to forty hours per week).

There is an obvious drawback, however. Finding skilled personnel is hard; finding multi-skilled personnel is even harder. More to the point, finding multi-skilled personnel willing to work flexible hours per week is what we might call 'mission impossible'.

Super7 solves this problem with ease. (One of the reasons, perhaps, to call it 'super'.)

Flexibility in Skills

Flexibility in skills facilitates capacity planning

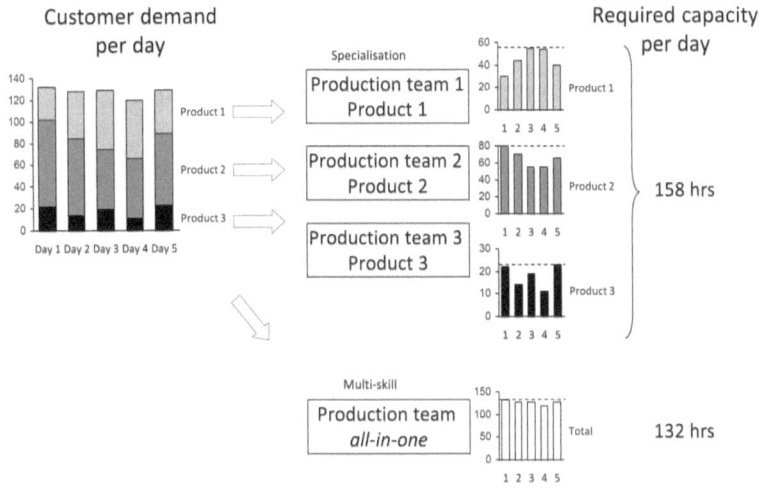

Figure 8

Super7 proposes aggregating skills through collaboration. A production unit consisting of a small group of people can be made multi-skilled by putting people with different skills together in one Super7. So, instead of demanding flexibility from the rare highly-skilled, multifaceted performers, a diverse team of separate skills is assembled to create a flexible and multifaceted collective that can then respond readily and in real-time to fluctuation, without putting any undue stress on one link in the chain.

Another benefit of the Super7 team structure? Learning on the job. When there is no more work within the Super7 for your particular specialty (or if you lack the one specialty that is required for the work that is left), what do you do? Do you go home, leaving your Super7 team to carry on without you?

No way – working with the team and *for the team* is the basic rule of the Super7. What happens in practice on a Super7 is that a colleague with a lot of work says, 'Come here, I'll show you how this works.' Team members are able to acquire new and necessary skills on the job. The advantage of applying this idea in an administration/ back office setting is that there are most likely no safety issues involved in this on-the-job, rapid dissemination of skills. In production, on the other hand, it could cause some safety issues – you wouldn't want someone learning to drive a forklift without a license, for example. In the back office setting, however, it's widely applicable. Before you know it, the entire Super7 is multi-skilled if the work requires that.

Learning on the job

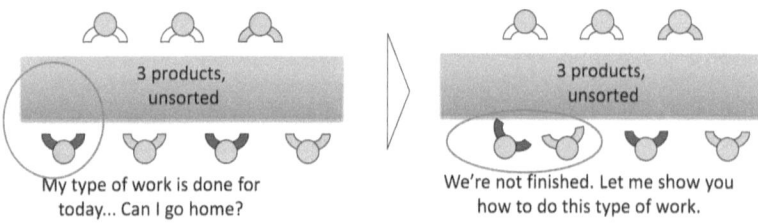

Figure 9

Flexibility in Capacity

Using flexible capacity to cope with fluctuation

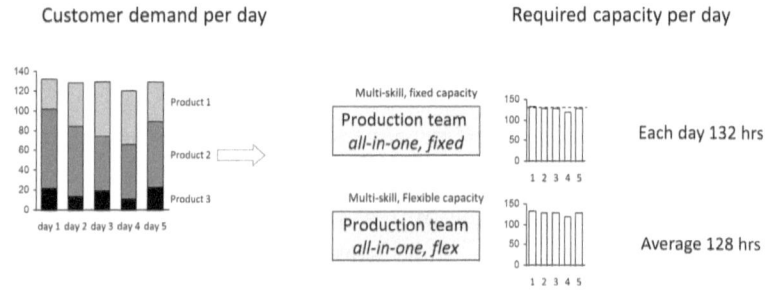

Figure 10

Capacity can be made flexible by letting the Super7 team size fluctuate between five and nine. This can either be done by using a fixed, multi-skilled team of five and adding flex workers who deal with the simpler work when needed to meet customer demands.

(Within the Netherlands, it's possible to find flex workers who are willing to work flexible hours, as long as you don't look for extraordinary skills.) A second solution within the Super7 model is to allow for the exchange of team members between Super7s. On days that are slow for one Super7 team, key members can be allocated to help another Super7 with higher demand on that day.

Examples of flexible capacity

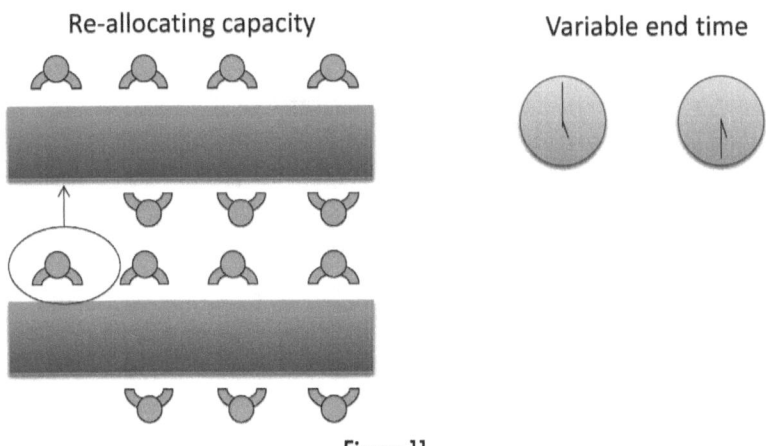

Figure 11

A team manager will typically have three or four Super7s under him or her. If one of the Super7s has capacity issues, the first possible solution is to move capacity from one Super7 to another. This requires a complete and up-to-date skills matrix, describing which employee can do what type of work, and to what level of maturity.

A skills matrix frames employees and tasks by listing employee names versus tasks, with four categories of skill levels:

0 = no skill
1 = can do skill but needs supervision
2 = can do skill within norm and without supervision
3 = can train others in this skill

In this way, Super7 allows for immediate and effective reallocation of resources, providing the flexibility needed to address fluctuation and avoid inventory.

Flow

Flow is another concept through which we can understand Super7 as the next logical step in the development of lean. During production, the product should be able to flow as easily as possible through the process — with no hiccups and no waiting and with the least amount of transport possible.

In one project I ran, a front office filled in a standardised, digital form, which the back office then typed over into the back-office system. The same fields, the same data. Why this transport from front to back office? Why the double work? Our solution: fill in the data just once, the front office fills out the back-office system, not the digital form.

Super7 helps flow because a customer request can be completely processed within one Super7, with no need for transport from one department to another. Teams are clustered from a process point of view, not from a specialism point of view. That means that if the process needs it, the Super7 teams are multidisciplinary.

Reason 3 : Supportive Management Style

Because eliminating micromanagement maximises flexibility and productivity

Putting Aside Micromanagement and Focusing on a Results-Oriented Managing Style

When I first arrived at OS Leeuwarden, management adhered to a 'classical' approach to driving productivity. A manager might delegate to employees by saying, 'You need to process this stack of work, within an hour' (so-called hour packages). They had optimised this approach for minimal costs by focusing on:

- making maximum use of the flexibility within the SLA in order to level the workload and minimise the need for overcapacity to deal with fluctuation
- leveraging standardised norms for how long an activity should take
- maximising individual productivity through hourly management of one-hour work packages.

The above was actually the result of implementing lean tools, such as heijunka (level-loading the factory), Pigeon-Box (hourly work packages), visual management (below-norm productivity is directly visible on the shop floor; i.e., package not finished in an hour), and standardised work (*standard* norms, *standard* duration, *standard* work instructions, etc.).

But then the rules changed. The throughput time in the SLA had become unacceptable to the bank's customers. In an era of real-time, online response, waiting two weeks for a checking account to become available was no longer acceptable to customers. The public opinion on banks shifted in a significant way – 'trustworthy financial institutions' became 'old-fashioned institutions'. As mentioned previously, the financial crisis, of course, did not help. Many customers began associating banks with the villains of the crisis, individuals intent on making themselves rich and taking the whole world down with them.

Assuaging customer fears and prejudices became key, and one of the best ways to do that was to limit throughput time. Thus, TITO became the new motto. This meant moving away from the cost minimum:

1. More capacity needed to cope with day-to-day fluctuations
2. Less management attention to productivity

The rub? The costs were actually *reduced*. Considerably. How was that possible?

Firstly, there were far fewer 'status calls' coming in from customers checking on their requests. Before, call centres were overrun with typical customer status checks (read: *complaints*) ;Did you receive the form I sent you?'; 'I haven't heard from ING for weeks now.'; 'I was wondering if something went wrong.'; and so on. A Dutch-language call centre is not an English-language call centre. It can't be handled by a large percentage of countries and workers. In other words, it isn't cheap to operate.

Secondly, customers now submitted far fewer double requests. In the past, when customers had concerns about the throughput time on their requests, they would often submit *additional* requests in an attempt to get satisfaction and/or responses, assuming that their original requests had somehow fallen through the cracks. This muddied the waters, racking up additional, unnecessary man hours. The shift to TITO eliminated much of the need for double requests, translating into fewer requests to process, and less capacity needed.

Super7 eliminated water spiders from the mix. This hidden

management layer of work distributors, which also included daily production planners responsible for managing inventory, was unnecessary with Super7 in place. Significantly, this non-value-added work was eliminated *without* having to increase capacity elsewhere.

Finally, productivity increased. Even with less management attention? Without hourly visual management? Let's look at that result in a bit more detail.

Productivity Increases with Super7

With a Super7 in place, the team is responsible for finishing all the work that comes in that day. There is enough capacity on average to keep them at optimum productivity levels, and capacity can be adjusted so that every day there is roughly enough capacity to cope with the work.

Of course, there will be busy days and quiet days. At the beginning of the day, the Super7 commits itself to finishing all the work for that day, or they ask for help from management. No help requested? It's up to the Super7 to figure out how to complete all of that day's work. This leads to significantly higher productivity on busy days. And, yes, significantly lower productivity on quiet days.

It is important, however, to note that this shows that the norms (how much time a certain type of request should take) contained slack. Norms always do. Both employees and management have incentives to prevent norms from being too strict. Employees like to be able to take a breath every now and then, and management is rewarded for always adhering to the SLA.

Implementing Super7 showed that productivity could be quite a bit higher on busy days.

What to do, then, about the quiet days? Our first idea was that a Super7 could be asked to send home some of the flex workers – those whose contracts allowed for variable workweeks, between twenty and forty hours per week. A second option was having regular employees take half a day off, using their vacation days.

What was interesting was that, in practice, the team often preferred to stick together. 'If we're in this together on busy days, we're in this together on quiet days. If you don't want to go home, you stay.' Flex workers could use the extra income from working more hours. And regular employees could save their vacation days if they wanted.

Enter 'output management'. I was first introduced to this principle by Filip Vandendriessche[7] at a Young Executive Program seminar. Essentially, output management means: you can leave workflow decisions up to your employees, as long as you *judge them on the results*. It is important to understand that management is still responsible for setting the boundary conditions; i.e., how much time can be allotted for a project, or how much full-time equivalent (FTE) can be used to come up with a solution to a particular problem.

At ING OS Leeuwarden, this principle translated to: TITO is the output that needs to be managed. Management was to help the team if they asked for assistance, but, otherwise, the Super7 itself determined how they would do the work. The manager also needed to set the boundary conditions; i.e., how many resources were available each day? This meant managers needed to engage in resource planning and forecasting the volume of work:

1. Using historical data of volumes to create a forecast for the coming two-week period. Forecast models used included:
   • volume from the previous year for the same period
   • averages of the previous four weeks
   • linear extrapolation of a trend over the previous four weeks.
   Forecast then became a managerial decision, based on expertise and the data from the three forecast models, above.

2. Planning the resources based on the forecast. Flex employees were told in advance when they would be needed in the coming two-week period.

3. Allowing the team to do the work and being available to assist the team during the day. The manager could add resources if the team 'pulled the alarm cord' (in lean terminology: 'Andon') and stated, 'We're not going to make it.'

This third point is illustrated nicely by the following anecdote. In the year after the implementation of Super7, managers from other departments frequently visited OS Leeuwarden, wanting to learn more about Super7. On one such visit, an OS team manager explained what was happening that day: one of his Super7s had a quiet day, while another Super7 in his team was quite busy. The visitor asked why the manager hadn't moved one person from the quiet Super7 to the busy Super7. 'Well, that's what I used to do, but not anymore. The busy Super7 hasn't asked me for help. I'm here to help, but only when I'm asked to.'

1. Evaluating forecast accuracy: Was the forecast too tight? Which forecast model was most accurate?
2. Evaluating a TITO (output) score: Too many green lights are *bad!*

Continuous improvement: raising the bar

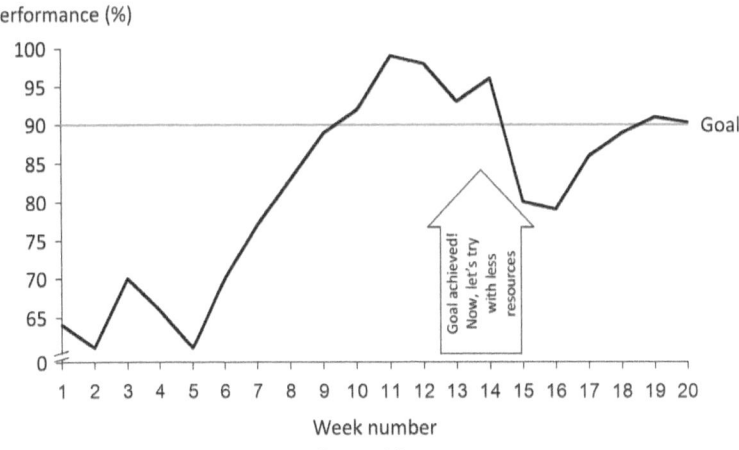

Figure 12

33

This point relates to a quote that is sometimes attributed, perhaps anecdotally, to a manager from Toyota: 'No problem is a problem.' I first heard this quote from Rob van Stekelenborg, a former mentor of mine at IG&H consulting, who had previously been responsible for the lean programme within Valeo, a French tier-1 automotive supplier to Toyota.

In the context of OS Leeuwarden, this meant that achieving four weeks in a row without any disruptions in TITO (no 'pulls on the alarm cord', no work shifted to the next day) was a signal first to celebrate a success, and then to make it *more challenging*: less resources, tighter capacity planning in the weekly planning/ forecasting cycles. So four weeks of green lights in the bigger picture equalled a red light.

3. Maintaining ongoing momentum and continuous improvement. A manager needed to readjust, constantly seeking higher average productivity through better setting of boundary conditions for a Super7.

Performance management is still an essential part of the new way of managing. The team should regularly stop to think: How did we do last period? What went right, what went wrong? And how can we improve on this for the next period? This requires accurate registration of performance data and up-to-date reporting of performance on the shop. At OS Leeuwarden, each team has a computer screen on the wall on which the performance can be shown. At the end of every workday, all work is administrated and registered into a performance management tool. A big plus of doing the administration at the end of the workday is that the customer doesn't have to wait; registration used to be done before the actual work, but now the customer receives help first.

A reporting system creates specific reports for each team. The team gets to see their team performance, and they can zoom in on how they did on a specific type of customer request. Each team has a weekly stand-up meeting around the performance screen, at which time they agree on necessary improvements, based on the facts about the performance. The team manager helps the team to understand the performance figures, but lets the team draw their own conclusions.

Standardised Work — An Important Part of Lean

Standardised Work: Standards as starting point for improvement

- Introduce standards for process, performance, and shop floor. Standard is the best that we can achieve at this moment (not necessarily good enough, but, nevertheless, our standard at this moment).
- Make deviations from standards visible; e.g., make sure that you can see that tools are missing, make sure that you can see that the machine settings are correct, make it impossible not to notice defects.
- Standardise reaction to deviations from standard: e.g., the assembly line is stopped when a problem is found in one step, the problem is corrected, and an improvement is started to prevent reoccurrence.
- Update the standard: each improvement focuses on removing waste from the value chain or preventing waste from occurring in the future. Each improvement leads to a new standard, and the cycle starts again.

CHAPTER 4

What Super7 Means for the Manager

All the aspects of Super7 involve quite a change in the daily work of the manager. We'll look at this in greater detail throughout this chapter, but the essential changes appear in the next three paragraphs.

First of all, managers go from setting their own priorities to following the rhythm of the work on the shop floor. Why should daily management of a production unit, which does repetitive work, not be repetitive? Through standardisation and lean manufacturing, the work of a production unit has been made more repetitive in the last years. It seems logical – and it is, in fact, common practice in automotive production – that the work of the operational manager is repetitive. Within banks, this is not common practice. Managers often see themselves as troubleshooters, or people coaches, or 'just doing this for the management experience on my way to the top' – they seldom see themselves as operational managers.

Next, managers go from sitting in meetings to being on the shop floor. By organising a stand-up meeting of a couple of minutes every day at the same time, the shop floor knows that there is no need to panic or to go find the manager in case of a production hiccup: they know the manager will be there in one hour exactly, they know that stand-up is at the right time to allow the manager to find a solution (i.e., that there is then even enough time to escalate to the highest manager the same day), and they know that until stand-up time, they (the team) know what to do. (For instance, if no production is possible, do a mini kaizen.)

Finally, managers go from less managing to more delegating. Let's take a deeper look at this in practice via a series of examples. Before Super7 implementation, assigning the work to teams required a lot of managing. With Super7, there is now less management of inventory, less management of assigning work, less management of skills, and less management of work in progress.

Management of Inventory

Prior to Super7, all work packages needed to be booked in the inventory management system, and the age of the inventory (i.e., when did we receive the customer request?) needed to be monitored and compared to the SLA. Then, if the system indicated, 'orange', i.e., 'we've got only one day left within SLA', priorities needed to be reshuffled urgently to prevent 'red' the next day.

Management of Assigning Work

Because there is a lot of work in inventory, team managers attempted to get the 'best work streams' assigned to their team. The norms for each work stream differed; moreover, not all norms set were accurate. Consequently, managers knew after a while which work streams caused them trouble ('Your team didn't meet the norm yesterday!'), and which work streams had a more lenient norm ('Good job, all work is finished well within the norm!').

Management of Skills

In the past, there was a daily production meeting in which the team managers, all together, determined which team would be doing which work streams the next day. In Super7s, this whole circus isn't needed. Each Super7 knows what work they will be doing: the same work every day, and all the work that came in that day. To prevent boredom and/or loss of skills as a result of the standard work for every Super7, people are exchanged between Super7s for a couple of days every now and then.

Management of Work In Progress

Before Super7, if there was a question about a certain type of work, the physical customer request needed to be found. But where was it? First, a manager needed to check the inventory system: is the work still waiting, or is it work in progress? A manager also needed to look in the report of the daily production meeting: where was the work assigned to? Finally, a request had to be submitted to the water spider: to whom did you give this work package? Super7 makes this much easier: work is always directly work In progress – no more inventory. A manager who knows what type of request it is also knows where it is: on the desk of that Super7.

A short note on office space here can point out another benefit of Super7: optimised office space. Each Super7 has their own office space. In OS Leeuwarden, the whole office interior was redesigned to give each Super7 their own recognisable shared office space, seven (or eight, in fact) desks close together (like a dinner table) with a lot of visibility, inviting colours, modern design office furniture, etc. Not only a more productive layout, but a very cool place to work now as well!

Lean Management

A while ago, I was walking around the shop floor of a food packaging firm, together with one of the team managers. We came to a packaging line where bell peppers were packaged three in one package. The machine was turning out packages; nothing much to see, really. I asked the manager: 'Is this machine running optimally?'

'It looks okay, we do have a lot of rejects, I think. . .' he answered. So I persisted: 'Is the machine setting okay? Does this machine have different settings at all?'

'Well, you can adjust the machine to fit the average size of the bell pepper. Basically, you can have a batch of small, medium, or large peppers.'

'Which are these?' I asked.

'Let me see. . . . . .these are small.'

'And the machine setting, is it set to "small"?'

The manager got a ladder, climbed to the top of the machine, looked at some dial or lever of some sort, and yelled down to the production staff: 'Stop the line! The machine is still on "large"!'

I suggested that they paint the lever bright yellow, so you could see it from the ground, and make clear labels for 'small', 'medium', and 'large', so that you could see how the machine was set from the shop floor. The production team did just that, and the machine performance was improved considerably.

The manager wasn't in control of the situation. How could he be? He couldn't see whether the machine was running correctly or not. And if he couldn't see, the machine operators probably couldn't, either. In any case, he wasn't able to help his team.

Back offices are often even less transparent. Sure, there are dashboards (often, lots of them), but the truth is out there, on the shop floor. In any operations department that is managed in a Lean manner, you will be able to see if the operation is running smoothly. If you can see it, the manager can see it, and then the manager will at least have the opportunity to manage.

In one back office, I asked the manager, 'Did your team have a good day or a tough day today?' She seemed a bit annoyed: 'How am I supposed to know? The reports come in next Monday.' Not in control, it would seem.

At OS Leeuwarden, any team manager asked will know the answer: 'Yes, two of my Super7s say they are going to make it, and one even expects to finish early. Another Super7 needs to have a couple of hours help at the end of the day.' He knows because he has asked the Super7s, and he can see for himself by the amount of work on the shop floor or in the inbox.

SECTION 2

Case Studies – Experiences with Super7 within ING

I n this section of the book, we will to look at some real-world results from implementing Super7 at ING, specifically: the one-year follow-up of Super7 at ING, the mortgages department's implementation of Super7, and the Credit Cards & Loans Department's implementation of Super7. These case studies will provide a clear picture of the transformation that can happen when Super7 replaces older lean techniques in the financial services sector.

I think you'll see from the results illustrated in the case studies of Chapters 5, 6, and 7 that Super7 is more than capable of addressing many of the issues facing financial services today. And perhaps you'll find some ideas for how Super7 can address and transform your own organisation. Even though these case studies involve ING-exclusive applications of Super7, I feel confident that you'll glean from them how applicable Super7 could be in a much wider array of financial services situations.

Let's take a look at Super7 at work within the financial services sector.

CHAPTER 5

OS Leeuwarden: One Year after Super7 Implementation

This chapter's case study looks at OS Leeuwarden one year after the initial deployment of Super7. Let's see whether TITO remained realistic, how much Super7 saved ING in terms of costs, and what other accessory benefits ING experienced as a result of Super7. We'll also look at the adjustments that had to be made – both from managerial and employee standpoints – in order to get the most potential out of the Super7 system.

When Fred Tuininga, the senior manager at OS Leeuwarden, first heard of our idea for a Super7 pilot in his organisation, he wasn't sure that it would be possible. Achieving TITO within the existing budget at Leeuwarden seemed difficult; achieving TITO at a *lower* budget seemed impossible. As the pilot project began, Tuininga expected costs to increase. But he supported the pilot nonetheless, because he realised that TITO delivery was what customers demanded.

One year after implementation, costs are actually lower because Super7 has created a new way of working on the shop floor. Double work has been reduced, and the back office no longer receives multiple requests from customers who are concerned that their first request (or more than one request) was ignored or lost in the shuffle.

The team also succeeded in reducing the amount of administrative work involved in all tasks.

Currently, OS Leeuwarden has expanded their hours of operation to match the hours of their branches and call centre: from 8 a.m. to 8 p.m. Any digital request received before 7 p.m. is processed the same day. There are no formal shifts: management asks employees who are willing to work a later schedule to take on the task. They have enough people who prefer a late schedule that this has balanced out optimally. It still sometimes happens that the actual workload is higher than expected. Almost always, though, this can be solved by employees working overtime. There isn't a formal registration of this: the Super7 team members decide amongst themselves how to compensate these hours with free time on quiet days. There is no formal registration of these hours. If the overtime becomes structural, they will indicate this to their manager. The manager can use the performance data to see whether extra capacity is needed. In one case, the Super7 asked for more capacity. Analysis of performance data showed that the workload hadn't increased, but, rather, that the productivity had been dwindling. The team recognised that they used to be able to do the work without structural overtime, and they drew their own conclusion: we need to step up our game.

Most days, OS Leeuwarden only needs a couple of employees to process the incoming requests between 6 p.m. and 8p.m. On Mondays, the busiest day of the week, it's a different story. In order to achieve TITO on Mondays, when all customer requests from the weekend need to be addressed, the work schedule had to be tweaked a bit: for most teams, Monday start times are now at 11.30 a.m., with the workday ending at 8 p.m. In this way, the Super7s are able to process the requests from the branches, which are delivered at around 12.30 p.m., as well as all the digital requests received during each weekend and early on every Monday.

Because of developments in automation – digital forms, digital straight-through processing, etc. – a pivotal reorganisation was necessary. This involved saying goodbye to a portion of the fixed staff. Of course, this was done in close cooperation with the Works Council. According to Tuininga, 'It's essential to involve the Works Council as early as possible in these situations. They need to be confident that the process is done thoroughly.'

The employees that stayed were selected based on whether they adapted to the new way of working. They had to respond positively to these questions: Are you willing to work according to the new opening hours? Can you be flexible in working hours, to a certain extent? In this way, Leeuwarden has created a culture that naturally needs to work TITO.

Moving forward, Leeuwarden is working on a project to increase productivity even further (specifically, by 10 per cent), through better planning and forecasting, including planning less overcapacity.

The shift in customer feedback over the first year of implementation has been dramatic. Tuininga believes that TITO is the reason for that. And while TITO is the crux of solving customer dissatisfaction, Super7 is the prerequisite, in Tuininga's opinion. He further believes that you can't ask a team of twenty to make their own decisions on work distribution or working late. Autonomous teams only work if the team is small enough to allow members to keep an eye on each other and have open communication. All employees were trained in how to give and receive feedback to facilitate this process.

There was some employee resistance during the transition: new opening hours meant a change in the balance of work/private time. Communication was key in handling this situation, as management had to explain why the new schedule was necessary, how it would benefit the customers, etc. In the end, everybody was convinced that it was necessary – not something everybody was happy about, but necessary nonetheless.

Another staffing issue arose along the way. Teams had to make sure they had enough capacity until 8 p.m., and each Super7 planned on the safe side. As a result, one year following implementation, there is often too much capacity between 6 and 8 p.m. Team managers now need to learn to plan the capacity a bit closer to forecast, and plan per day, not just the capacity for after 6 p.m. They might also need to combine the 'safety capacity' from all teams – not one hour extra in each team, but one hour extra capacity available in total.

Cultural Shifts with Super7, One Year In

One year after the implementation of Super7, OS Leeuwarden has experienced a cultural shift from being process oriented to customer oriented. Best example: if customers can send requests until 7 p.m. through the branches, Leeuwarden processes them until 8 p.m.

According to one consultant involved in OS Leeuwarden, 'In the past, people talked about "pieces" (short for pieces of work) when referring to customer requests. Now they say "customers". In fact, within some teams, you have to put a Euro in the team pot when you say "piece" in reference to a customer request.'

Super7 implementation has resulted in some interesting shifts for management as well. Tuininga has had to learn to let go. When he encounters a problem now, he needs to stop and think: is this something the Super7 can solve on their own? In the past, managers were accustomed to solving any problems themselves. Management now needs to stimulate the Super7 to solve the problem themselves, by facilitating the process and asking the right questions. 'Creating the right culture starts with ourselves… and it's rewarding when the Super7 does solve their own problems,' according to Tuininga

Tips and Tricks, One Year In

Work TITO *because of your customers*. Do it for your customers, not primarily for the costs, and not primary for your employees. Do it to provide the service they deserve. The other results may be extra benefits, but they shouldn't be the main goal. Super7s – small teams – are a prerequisite for giving more responsibility to the teams and for achieving TITO.

Explain, explain, explain. Explain the new approach to everyone – to all employees on the shop floor, to the team managers, and so on – and always with the same consistent message: 'We do it for our customers. TITO is the only way that we can give our customers the service they deserve.' In the beginning, there were employees that reasoned, 'It's bad for me, and therefore it must be bad for the customer.' Show the effects, especially on customer satisfaction, NPS, and the number of 'status calls' (i.e., 'Did you receive my request? I haven't heard from ING in weeks!').

Pace yourself, and adjust as needed. When you start working TITO, you may only be able to achieve it for 80 per cent of the volume. In order to achieve 100 per cent, you may have to change the number of hours in the workday. (Changing the working hours proved inevitable at ING). Start with a pilot, which will show that this way of working does work. Keep trying: don't cast every change in stone; allow for changes in teams, work distribution, working times, etc. Yes, running a lot of pilots can make things complicated, but it is usually essential to success.

Managers, set the boundary conditions, but don't make all decisions on the 'how' yourselves. Let's consider this example: During the holiday season, OS Leeuwarden expects a lower volume of customer requests. A lot of the employees, moreover, want to take vacation around Christmas. Prior to this year, management decided that a maximum of 60 per cent of the employees could take vacation. Management collected all vacation requests for that period, approving them as long as capacity was over 40 per cent of normal capacity. This year, management has decided to try a different approach: Team managers tell the Super7s the expected volume – the forecast – for the holiday season. This roughly amounts to 40 per cent of the normal volume. Managers then tell the team that TITO needs to be maintained. They ask the Super7 to come up with a solution; i.e., who takes time off when, etc. It's the Super7's responsibility to determine time off; as long as they keep working TITO, the time off will be allowed and approved.

It's not impossible. According to a consultant involved in optimising forecasting in OS Leeuwarden, 'All team managers said beforehand, "My team's work is so unpredictable that forecasting is useless." But after a couple of months, the figures show differently: forecasting accuracy is quite good, often within 5 per cent of the actual volume.'

Facilitate. Don't push the team towards solutions. The strength of the Super7 is its autonomy, so work to guide it towards answers, but allow the team to discover those answers for themselves. Be there on the shop floor. Be there when the team discusses how they are going to do the work that day. Take an active part in the conversation; be a presence, but leave the ultimate decision making up to the team. The same goes for the weekly performance-improvement meetings. Show the team the facts about performance, but let them draw their own conclusions.

Do what your customer asks you to do. TITO is only needed if your customer asks for this. However, if the customer demands TITO for one type of request, it makes sense to start working TITO on all requests: process all requests the same, and standardise the way of working. According to Tuininga, 'Working without inventory of course has additional benefits: inventory demand valuable management attention, registration, recounting etc. But these benefits are secondary to meeting the demands of our customers.'

Employee Feedback, One Year In

With all the flexibility ING asks from their OS Leeuwarden employees, it might be interesting to see what the employees have to say about all the changes. After one year of implementing Super7, an employee survey was conducted.

A great majority of the employees now feel that they are part of a team. This is a slight but significant shift from the year before, when more employees scored neutral in response to this question.

The teams indicate that communication between colleagues is

open and honest; only 10 per cent disagreed. Good communication is vital within Super7, for solving problems, giving each other feedback, etc. This comes as no surprise, really: otherwise, how could the teams have performed as well as they did within the new way of working?

What is one of the most important lessons culled from Super7? According to Tuininga, 'Understanding that we are doing this for our customers.'

Did this have the desired result? A major improvement was recorded since the moment of implementation. Now, after one year, no more than 20 per cent of the employees disagree that TITO was the right approach to improve customer satisfaction. Still quite a number, but the number disagreeing is almost half of what it was at the time of initial implementation.

And what happened in regard to the sense of individual responsibility? In the past, people were responsible for their own work only, whereas now they share the responsibility for TITO within a Super7. The employee survey responses were clear about this: almost 100 per cent of employees agreed, to a certain extent, that the implementation of TITO with Super7s made a greater appeal to their individual responsibility.

The way employees view management has changed too. The survey recorded a great improvement on employees' perceived support from management.

Finally, the work-life balance also came up on the survey. With the newly introduced workday of 12.30 p.m. to 8 p.m. on Mondays, as well as the new work schedules (from 8 a.m. to 8 p.m.), management expected some employee dissatisfaction. The results from the survey question 'Do you experience a good balance between work and private life?' showed that more employees have experienced deterioration in work-life balance. But, on the other side, the number of employees indicating a good work-life balance had also increased. In short, the number of positives was larger than the number of negatives. The majority used to vote 'neutral' on this statement; now the opinions were more polarised, more outspoken.

It's always a good idea to ask employees for their opinion. A regular survey gives valuable insight on how the Super7s are doing, what's on people's minds, how they view management, etc. There will always be a couple of loud complainers within a group (within the Netherlands, this is certainly true), but a survey gives you the chance to hear everybody. And for OS Leeuwarden, the survey results indicate that management is on the right track with Super7.

CHAPTER 6

Super7 at the Mortgages Department

In this chapter, we'll examine another case: implementation of Super7 within the mortgages sector of ING. The mortgage business had, of course, experienced a huge shift during the global financial crisis, incurring marked changes in both customer perception and in-house processes at ING. Our Super7 implementation had to compensate for rather significant staff cutbacks while also compensating for decreasing customer loyalty and satisfaction.

The mortgages department of ING that we will look at in this case study was a medium-size organisation, with around 180 full-time employees working on processes and about 40 full-time employees in support staff and management positions. The tasks on the shop floor primarily involved processing customer change requests on existing mortgages. This included basic issues (e.g., an address change or a new checking account number), as well as higher-level requests (e.g., changing the type of mortgage or adjusting a sum). Both the basic and higher-level requests were daily tasks.

Because of recent difficulties in the mortgages market caused by the financial meltdown, the volume of customers at the firm was on the decline. As a result, the mortgages department was planning on reducing full-time employees in an attempt to control costs. Productivity was in good shape, at the time, with productivity measures coming in consistently at around 100 per cent, and with work typically completed on time. However, there was a feeling within management that it was never really busy, and that it was never really a stretch to achieve 100 per cent productivity.

We approached the implementation of Super7 with this key question in mind: how much efficiency potential could be achieved with the implementation of process improvements?

Our objective was to find sufficient potential to compensate for a 12 per cent reduction in staff and to implement the required measures quickly and efficiently.

Implementing Super7

After our initial analysis, it seemed the potential for improving individual processes was just not big enough. This meant that the necessary improvements had to be found in two things: (1) reducing the non-productive time, and (2) improving all the processes in one go (i.e., the entire way of working).

So, our new key question was: how would we reduce non-productive time and increase productivity for all processes?

In the past, ING had chosen to address these kinds of questions by instituting even tighter management, but at the time, the news of the Super7 success of Leeuwarden was going round within ING. Now there seemed to be two alternatives:

- more management, more steering, steeper targets
- output management: monitoring TITO performance, while step-wise reducing capacity, and giving the Super7 the freedom of *how* to achieve this TITO performance

The management team was excited about the new responsibility that Super7 offered for the shop floor. And they didn't like the prospect of increased steering: they felt that they were already doing this, so it would be more of the same at most.

Management of the mortgages department had visited OS

Leeuwarden prior to running their pilot. During that observation, they had noted that it was the combination of TITO, output management of TITO, and autonomous teams that made Super7 a success. In setting up the mortgages pilot, the team manager and support staff selected the suitable teams and work streams for the pilot and decided to install three Super7s.

By clustering work streams, management created enough work for three Super7s. For the full-time staff, this structure created more work than they were accustomed to, which would eventually compensate for the staff reduction. Employees and managers were trained, and we decided to go for TITO+1, meaning that they gave the work preparation team an additional day to digitise and prepare the work (i.e., upload it into the workflow management tool).

After that, it was go time. The results?

TITO+1 was achieved, even with the increased workload, and even on busy days. In addition, productivity registered at 100 per cent consistently. Two out of the three Super7s showed increased productivity, even on not-so-busy (average) days. One showed unchanged productivity on not-so-busy days.

What was particularly interesting was that *all* three Super7s showed impressive productivity on busy days, well above 100 per cent.

The benefits for the customers were pretty evident as well. Throughput times on requests were reduced to two days. Previously, customers had become accustomed to long wait times during the mortgage consideration process. That said, increased throughput times weren't really a customer requirement as such, but they did come as a very pleasant surprise.

For management, the potential of productivity increase as a result of Super7 was clear because of the achieved performance on busy days. This gave management confidence that the FTE reduction could be effectuated without damaging the customer service.

There were a few bumps in the road. One Super7 complained about one of the team members calling in sick too often. (All of the other team members of that Super7 voiced the same complaint). The problem was discussed within the team, and the pilot started with the same people, no alterations made.

More severely, the pilot team's manager didn't naturally change his way of managing the team. He delegated capacity problems, but he wasn't always available to help or escalate when needed. Also, the important task of planning to forecast wasn't done by the team manager, but by a staff department. This meant that the team manager didn't feel as involved as a manager should. During the pilot, this was compensated for by the fact that the consultant was there to aid the pilot team. Before broad implementation, however, this issue needed to be addressed. In the preparation of the roll-out, a lot of attention was given to the changing role of the manager. A specific training programme was developed, and it was decided to let consultants coach the managers during the first weeks of the new way of working.

Lessons Learned

One lesson made clear through this Super7 pilot was that it is crucial to give a lot of attention to the management: training on planning and forecasting is critical, but equally important is being available for escalation of problems during the day, solving capacity problems, shifting capacity between Super7s, etc.

It was also remarkable to see how the culture on the shop floor shifted after implementation. The shop floor was positive from day 1 – especially about being responsible for how to do the work during the day, who would do what, etc. This empowerment factor really transformed their attitudes about their tasks and the company in general.

Before, staff had been responsible for their own hour packages – and just that. Now, teams worked together, discussing who did what, etc. In general, they were proactive and engaged by their work. With the Super7 approach, on busy days, individuals could focus on tasks that they did most efficiently. And on quiet days, there was time for learning from each other, creating an enhanced sense of cooperation on the shop floor, and allowing the staff to get some variety in how they executed their tasks.

Moving forward, ING plans on rolling out Super7s for the entire mortgages department. Given the results of the pilot, it seems like a transition that will only increase productivity and enhance the business culture of this organisation.

CHAPTER 7

Super7 at the Credit Cards & Loans Department

In this chapter, we'll look at our third and final case study: Super7 implementation at the Credit Cards & Loans Department (CC&L) of ING. In this case, the stakes were just as high, with significant cutbacks scheduled for which Super7 had to pick up the slack. We were tasked with increasing throughput times while simultaneously implementing and maintaining TITO, in spite of these significant reductions to the staff.

The focus in this case study was on the administrative processes handled by the back office of CC&L. Basically, this entailed all the administrative tasks associated with accounts, except for the opening of new accounts – such services as requesting a PIN code, requesting a second card, and so on. Admin tasks addressed for loan accounts involved processing requests, such as a change of address or even ending a loan contract.

The back office itself was rather compact, with a relatively small number of full-time employees. The support staff consisted of water spiders who distributed the work to individual employees. The tasks were all processed in a very analogue way – information was culled from physical documents or printed e-mails, which staff then used to make changes to the back office's admin system by hand.

As stated, an impending cost-cutting measure which would reduce full-time employees was already in the works, promising to complicate and extend throughput times. The back office knew they had to take proactive steps to streamline their processes and reduce throughput times before the cuts took place.

The department was co-located with OS Leeuwarden, and the management at CC&L had heard of the Leeuwarden's success with TITO. The time parameters of the CC&L back office diverged from Leeuwarden's situation in a significant way – CC&L received customer requests until well into the evening (later than Leeuwarden did). Creating a TITO situation under these circumstances would take a bit of finessing. Implementing TITO, however, would make it possible to control the level of customer service after reducing FTE.

We did have a clear perspective on the central dilemma of the task at hand: how could we get to TITO, and then maintain TITO, with less personnel?

Setting Objectives and Goals

The main objectives of the project were:
- to eliminate backlog and start working TITO
- to continue working TITO once established
- to increase efficiency.

Our analysis of the status of the back office's existing processes showed that customer requests were often handled by more than one person, with each person only processing one specific part of the customer request. There was ample room for improvement where efficiency was concerned. It was decided that we would initiate a pilot Super7 and TITO at the CC&L back office.

There were several high-level goals set for the pilot from the beginning that we knew were a good fit with Super7. Firstly, efficiency needed improvement, but at the same time the organisation didn't want the management to say *how* things should be done. Secondly, it was important to shift the culture on the shop floor; not only did employees need to focus more on customer needs, they also needed to be more empowered in their work. Plus, the organisation wanted to reduce the hidden management layer of water spiders, eliminating these work distributors completely. Finally, and perhaps most importantly, the goal was to ensure that all customers would get their requests addressed in a timely manner, every time.

Organising the Pilot

We decided to start with Loans and then address Credit Cards a few weeks into the pilot, after new systems would have a chance to fall into place. The team size in Loans was such that it fitted within one Super7, both before and after the reduction.

First, we set about explaining the theory of Super7 Operations and TITO, including the 'how to manage' aspects: forecasting, capacity planning, letting the *how* be decided by the shop floor, managing output (TITO), and being available on the shop floor during the day to help (reallocate capacity) should the Super7 be in danger of not making TITO.

We also asked the team what they would need in place, logistically, to cope if we were to remove the water spiders. The team itself came up with a team board, on which the team could visualise who would be working on what that day.

Results

The results of the Loans pilot were pretty quick in coming. From day 2 of the pilot, we were able to achieve TITO – and maintain it. It became clear at once that the structure of the Super7 had the efficiency needed to maintain TITO, despite the late-day customer requests.

Even after the FTE reduction took place, TITO was still on track, and the team was still operating with sufficient efficiency.

The benefits for the Loans section were myriad. Throughput time was reduced to within one day. Plus, this was done with the elimination of a water spider, delivering some cost reduction to the organisation. There was one unexpected and rather enlightening benefit: ideas started bubbling up from the shop floor. The Super7 started coming up with their own notions for improvement, such as using a different tool for doing calculations. This shift in culture was significant. The team owned their work and took charge of improving it. A big part of this may have been facilitated by two things: (1) involving a Black Belt who was proactive in asking questions, and (2) having management's thorough attention throughout the pilot. Regardless, the staff was definitely engaged with their tasks in a way they had not been before.

Lessons Learned

One problem that presented itself did need a bit of finessing. Within the team, there was one senior employee. At the beginning, it proved difficult to give responsibility for 'who does what' to the team: the others would naturally look at the senior person to tell them what to do. And he naturally acted as a kind of foreman or team manager. It took some time for the team (and some additional training and coaching for the senior), before the team was able to make decisions as a team and work as a unit. Today, the senior isn't the spokesperson during meetings with the manager, and he encourages all team members to speak up.

An important lesson can be distilled from this problem: having a leader within a Super7 may complicate their cooperation. It seems to work better when a Super7 consists of equals.

Another issue is that of incentives: the department didn't adjust the target setting for their employees. If you work as a team, should you have targets and incentives based on team performance? I strongly believe that financial team incentives can play an important role in making the final step towards continuous improvement. Several publications, especially on effectiveness of operational excellence teams (e.g., total productivity maintenance [TPM] teams, autonomous teams, Six Sigma project teams, etc.), confirm that team incentives are more effective than individual targets. However, individual targets also have their merits, and a combination of team and individual targets may well be worth considering. Moreover, targets and incentives aren't the only driver (or even the main driver) for success of Super7 teams, and they should be part of an integrated approach.

Credit Cards Pilot

After a few weeks, the set-up and results of the Loans pilot were shared with the Cards team. The team was enthusiastic, and a similar pilot was prepared there.

Right from go, the Cards pilot proved a different kettle of fish: to start with, Cards had more backlog. Additionally, there were many money transfer transactions in the log of tasks in this department. These types of transactions would be impossible to get to TITO, especially when transfers were initiated to outside banks.

A week into the pilot, however, we were almost at TITO. Unfortunately, after the FTE reduction, backlog began growing again. There were a couple of issues involved here. The daily stand-ups, which were necessary for the manager to help in case of problems, weren't well organised. It took some time before the management got into the rhythm and discipline.

Some resistance to the new processes surfaced right after the FTE reduction as well, with staff complaining that they were understaffed. The reason for this became clear soon enough, however. The consultant found, quite by coincidence, that a couple of new employees had started at the same time that the FTE reduction took place. The problem wasn't understaffing, it was low efficiency. The new employees were still learning the work, and they lacked the skills and speed necessary to keep efficiency where it needed to be. As soon as their training was completed, the backlog was eliminated, and TITO was maintained – all without adding more people.

Another issue that surfaced was that the Cards Super7 required more specialisation. Not every member of the team could do all the work, making the Super7 somewhat less flexible. We were able to address this during the pilot by simply changing the rules. The requirement was based on old rules that we didn't have to adhere to in the Cards Super7 implementation.

A Shift in Culture

In the end, one of the most significant results of the CC&L pilot was the shift in culture on the shop floor. The employees now felt responsible for the customers. They were also taking the initiative to source their own ideas and help improve the system, as with their invention of the white board for visualising work division. Across the board, the employees at CC&L have become more productive as a result of the implementation of Super7, and they enjoy the part they play in addressing the 'how' of their work.

SECTION 3

Super7 Outside of Operations –
Ideas and Experiments

n this section of the book, we will discuss ways in which Super7 can work outside of operations. By exploring the ideas and experiments provided as examples, you will be able to develop your own plan for real-world design and implementation of Super7 within your own organisation.

CHAPTER 8

Super7 within a Small Consultancy Team

Super7 and its core principles have proved successful in several environments, but always ones that naturally lend themselves to a team ethos. It seemed that it would be valuable to implement and test the concept of Super7 in an environment that *didn't* lend itself to a team ethos, and then see how things worked out.

In this chapter, we're going to look at an experiment I conducted in order to see whether you can create excellence through teamwork in a consultancy environment. Before we get to that, though, let's take a moment to look at what cooperative excellence is exactly.

For many years, manufacturing plants have benefited from small, highly specialised operations that work in close cooperation to form the product, a model that epitomises excellence in operation. Super7 is nothing more than people working together in small teams and in close cooperation, in order to achieve operational excellence.

I believe that a team can perform extremely well and reach a performance level that exceeds the performance level of each of the individuals that make up the team, a belief that has only been confirmed through my experience developing Super7. Provided, that is, that the team has the right mix of talented individuals/ interdisciplinary experts who agree to help each other out.

A question that came up for me, however, was whether this was actually possible in a consultancy environment. Could a team of consultancy experts actually increase the quality of their individual assignments by applying the concepts of cooperative excellence?

I set out to prove that consultants – who, in this case, work individually or with a project team from the client – could increase the quality of their individual assignments.

There were nine people in the team, including me. Everyone involved was between the ages of twenty-nine and forty, and well-qualified in their respective disciplines. Each of us was assigned a project with a duration ranging from one to nine months. These were typical operational management and operational business intelligence projects, such as:

- redesigns of customer processes
- realisations of end-to-end measurements of operational performance dashboards
- functional project support on implementation project for dashboard tooling.

Objectives

I had multiple objectives in place with this project. Naturally, I wanted to achieve more cooperation within the team. More to the point, I wanted to create an environment that fostered a shared sense of direction for the team as a whole. This in turn would ideally lead to an enhanced focus on team targets, thereby directly influencing the success of the team. I also wanted to increase both the effectiveness and the usefulness of our biweekly team board stand-ups.

As in enterprise, this entire exercise posed a few complications/obstacles from the get-go.

Earlier attempts at introducing visual management had failed to improve employee engagement, mainly because there was no direct influence – as a team – on the targets monitored. We were all convinced that team board stand-up sessions continually prove useful for our clients in our projects, and that if implemented well, they could improve both the success of the project and the engagement of the team members. It would, however, be a hard fit because work in consultancy is far less repetitive, and there are no common goals.

The Solution

At this point in this narrative, I don't think you'll be too surprised by my solution: I wanted the consultants to help each other by contributing to each other's projects. But how could this possibly work in consultancy? Let's look at it in detail.

In a particular project, there may be an activity that the consultant (Consultant A) performs adequately. That is, while the consultant performs this particular activity pretty satisfactorily, he or she does not excel in it. At the same time, another consultant (Consultant B) may excel in the same activity. Naturally, the project will benefit if Consultant B helps Consultant A with this activity.

It's important to understand that, as a part of the experiments, when consultants don't like doing a particular activity, or have to do something they're not good at, they can't ask for help. (Theoretically, they could ask for help, but that is not part of the experiment.) The idea is for consultants to help by utilising their individual strengths. Thus, Consultant A must ask for help *only* if it will allow Consultant B to use his or her own strength.

I based the whole thing on a simple idea: every consultant has a unique ability (or abilities), or an activity that he or she excels in. The whole team will benefit if each consultant can make more use of his or her unique ability. This will work, because as and when the consultant works on an activity using his or her unique ability, individual efficiency increases, and the average time taken to complete the activity also increases.

For a few of my colleagues, putting down their unique abilities on paper was difficult. You would be surprised, in general, just how difficult this can be for many people.

What could a unique ability or talent be in this context? It could be anything that a consultant excels in: structuring large amounts of data, delivering a message (in a presentation, for example), designing creative approaches and solutions, analysing stakeholders and stakeholder management, analysing data problems, or creating a storyline.

This process of self-assessment, combined with each team member bringing unique skills to the table, not only boosted the confidence of all involved but also increased teamwork (even though each person had a different project). It made consultants feel like they were a part of the team, more so than ever before.

The Pilot

At the kick-off session, I asked all the consultants to write down their unique abilities. I then stated that the duration of this pilot test would be three months. Three months of sharing abilities and learning. Once every two weeks, each consultant would identify activities that a colleague could help out with, enabling that colleague to use the needed unique ability to the fullest. We also decided to hold biweekly meetings to evaluate and discuss the time constraints that resulted from all the reshuffling of work.

The Result

After three months, we all met, and this is what we learned: in five instances, a colleague asked for help, which another colleague provided. In each instance, this increased the quality of the project, according to the consultants involved. Let's look at three of these instances in detail.

In the first case, one consultant asked another for help on a risk analysis of data errors within a Lean Six Sigma project. In the second case, a consultant requested help on designing the project approach in the Define phase of a Lean Six Sigma project. In the third case, a consultant asked for help in creating the storyline at the end of the Analyse phase of a Lean Six Sigma project.

In all three cases, the consultants who helped out by offering their respective unique abilities said the same thing: they enjoyed it very much, and they felt positive about the work, even though it was quite hard to find the time to help out their colleagues. Amongst the consultants who asked for help, all felt that their projects definitely benefited from the contributions made by their colleagues. (It bears mentioning here that a few of the consultants found it hard to find a suitable activity in their project that they could share with a colleague, especially on a regular basis.)

Overall, the experiment was a success. The pilot showed that cooperative excellence could be implemented in a consultancy environment – only in those instances, though, where it was possible to find a match between an activity and a unique ability. In hindsight, this difficulty in finding enough matches was the only thing that hindered the pilot. But in spite of all that, the pilot definitely showed potential, and proved that striving for excellence via the cooperation of a Super7 could work in many environments, even ones that would seem a counterintuitive fit at first.

CHAPTER 9

Is There a Use for Super7 Outside of Back Offices?

The use of Super7 (small teams) has proved crucial to creating the flexibility in capacity required to maintain TITO production in the back offices of ING. There might well be other areas where the same kind of flexibility would be of use. If, like me, you believe that people working closely together, making use of each other's strengths, can achieve more than they could separately, it may be interesting to find out if Super7 and TITO could be effective and successful in your own work.

At the moment of writing this book, I've been asked to help a department of product managers tasked with ensuring that end-to-end delivery of a product runs smoothly, improving the involved processes, and participating in all kinds of change projects regarding the product(s). The work of a product manager is highly specialised: in-depth knowledge of one or a couple of products is key to doing this job successfully. On the other hand, the high level of specialisation has made the department vulnerable to product managers falling ill or leaving the department – and taking their knowledge with them. Plus, when really large-scale projects are started, the involved product manager would often need to work full-time on project activities, making it impossible to work on other high-priority issues.

This organisation felt they needed flexibility, and that's when they called on me for help.

Could the work of seven product managers be done by one team of seven product managers? Or would that be no different than the current situation, with each product manager only handling an individual section of the work?

The solution lies in what the team is able to do for each other. The team is not able to do all the work together, so that's not an option. What they could do, however, is set priorities as a team, instead of each product manager setting priorities separately. It could be that the second priority of one of the product managers is more urgent, or has more customer impact, than the first priority of another product manager. Thus, it would become possible to assign capacity to what's most important to the team, instead of each product manager assigning capacity to his or her own top priority.

Another option would be to make sure that every product manager has at least one colleague that can replace him or her if needed. That would mean that the already highly specialised product managers would need to learn all the ins and outs of another product aside from their own. It's my understanding that this is similar to the current way that Toyota is working. At Toyota, each specialist needs to know at least three specialisms, and at least three persons need to be able to perform each specialism.

This example shows how you could look at your own situation. Start with asking yourself the question: what kind of help could team members give each other in this situation? In the case of simple work being done by a mono-skilled Super7, the team members can do each other's work, and they can also help each other in getting the work done. In multi-skilled Super7s, the team members of the same skill can help each other out, and the other team members will work on learning that skill when the other work is low. Plus, in Super7s where sequential process steps are taking place within the Super7 – for instance, when one person prepares the work and another does the final check – the team can help each other to keep pace with the slowest step, avoiding a build-up of work and keeping the work flowing without big piles of inventory.

The trick is to find what the team *as a team* can do for one another. The team needs to be able to respond to an issue as a team. If each team member has an individual project, an issue with that project will be the issue of that team member only. The others don't know enough about the project to help. Only when the others know what the project is about can they help.

The team also needs decision making power: the power to react to issues as a team. The team may be able to set priorities as a team, instead of each team member setting his or her own priorities. The team may be able to change the order of the work that is done within the team or the amount of work that is put into each project.

With Super7, some of the decision making power of the team comes from delegation from their team manager. However, there is a limit to what the team manager can delegate. Managers are still responsible and accountable for their departments; they take part in management team meetings, they can use their direct line of management for escalation, etc. These things can't be delegated to the team.

Sometimes, new degrees of freedom need to be added: more room for decision making, room that wasn't there before, even for the manager. For instance, a Super7 can decide to change their work schedule, while before, even the manager couldn't do that. To find the new degrees of freedom and new power for the team requires creativity and thinking outside the box. If you succeed in achieving this, however, you will get a whole new level of cooperation within your team. And, as we have seen, people that cooperate can achieve far more than the sum of their individual contributions. This is the essence of a successful team.

Another problem that needs to be addressed is that part of the work of each individual becomes invisible. When a team member helps a colleague to excel, the excellence of this colleague will show. But how can you see what that helping team member contributed? You can't. The helping team member sacrificed personal effort, time that could have gone to his or own project, for the benefit of the colleague. 'If you can't measure it, you can't manage it' is the common belief. If, however, you look closely at a team, if you as a manager are present on the shop floor, you will be able to see what is happening. You can see who is cooperating, who is taking the time to help others, and who is not. There may not be hard data as a result, but your observations should be just as valuable.

CONCLUSION

As I hope this book has conveyed, I'm very passionate about the principles of teamwork. It's one of the reasons why I've enjoyed my work so much and been able to develop Super7 Operations. Cooperating towards operational excellence and a supportive, output-focused management style are just a few of the things that drive me and inspire me in my work, and they all clearly play key roles in Super7 Operations.

From what we've discussed in this book, I hope that you now have a clear perspective on the transformative potential of Super7 Operations. With Super7 Operations, your organisation can experience all of the core benefits that Super7 has demonstrated again and again, including realigning business culture to focus on the customer, reducing inventory, and creating a more supportive and more effective management structure. As you begin experimenting with Super7 Operations in your own environment, you may well uncover even more benefits of this approach through your own implementations and creativity.

I now look forward to testing new waters with Super7 Operations in order to get an even broader perception of its potential. To keep up with the conversation as it develops, you can follow my work and join the discussion at www.super7ops.com. I hope that I've transferred a bit of my enthusiasm to you, and that you are as excited about Super7's potential as I am.

As you move forward with your own experiments with Super7 Operations, I would very much like to hear from you via our website.

Collaboration and feedback is at the core of what I do, and I would love to establish a dialogue with others as they initiate their own implementations of Super7. By working together and exploring new directions for this exciting approach to lean, we could create some productive and dynamic new momentum for our industry and beyond.

REFERENCES

1. BCG, *Special Report – Rethinking Lean: Beyond the Shop Floor* (Nov. 2009).
2. James P Womack, Daniel T Jones, *Lean Thinking* (2nd rev. upd. edn., New York: Simon & Schuster, 2006).
3. Scrum.org, *Scrum Guide* (last accessed Sept. 2013); InformIT. com, *Scrum, Agile Practices, and Visual Studio* (last accessed Sept. 2013); *Disciplined Agile Delivery in a Nutshell* (last accessed Sept. 2013).
4. Stephen P. Robbins, Timothy A. Judge, *Essentials of Organizational Behavior* (12th edn., New Jersey: Prentice Hall, 2013).
5. Joseph Pelrine, *Coaching Self-Organizing Teams*, SPA 2009 Conference (April 5-8, 2009).
6. Ringelmann, M., 'Recherches sur les moteurs animés: Travail de l'homme' ['Research on animate sources of power: The work of man'], *Annales de l'Institut National Agronomique*, 2/12 (1913), 1–40.
7. Filip Vandendriessche, Jef Clement, 'Leidinggeven zonder bevelen' ['Management without orders'], *LannooCampus/Scriptum* (2006).

ACKNOWLEDGEMENTS

I would like to thank everybody at ING who contributed to this book or to projects mentioned in this book. Especially Fred Tuininga and Bart Schlatmann, whose commitment to improving operations at the ING organisation made all of this possible. And all the managers at Operational Services (OS), who allowed all the experimenting within their department, and who played a major role in making it all happen. I would also like to thank my colleagues at ING – the Black Belts. Especially Wendell and Carmen, who supported me all the way during this process. And Robbert, Sander, Carly, Lesley, and Leefa, who all contributed to this book by sharing their experiences with me.

I would also like to thank Eleni Valasis for helping me with language, style, and editing. Finally, a big thank-you to my wife, Angie, and daughters, Amy and Lani, for being so patient with me while I was writing this book.

INDEX

implementation of Super7,
mortgages department case
study, 52–54
ING bank
Leeuwarden project. *See*
Leeuwarden (ING
branch)
new process, 12
old process, 10
previous customer-service
improvements, 11
Internet, impact of on customers'
expectations/experiences,
5–6, 29–30
inventory
management of, 38
means waiting, for
customers, 24
reduction of as benefit of
Super7, 15
requires resources/management
attention, 24
as type of waste, 7, 14
as way to cope with
fluctuation, 23

L

lean
basic steps of, 7
trend of in financial services, 6
true benefits of, xi
lean management, xii, 40
Lean Six Sigma, ix, xi, 68
Lean Thinking (Womack & Jones), 7
learning on the job, 25, 26
Leeuwarden (ING branch), 3, 5, 9,
11, 29, 32, 33, 34, 39
lessons learned
Credit Cards & Loans
Department's (CC&L)

implementation of
Super7, 60–61
mortgages department's
implementation of
Super7, 54–55
level-loading the factory
(heijunka), 29
logistics, part of new process, 12, 13

M

management
of assigning work, 38
of inventory, 38
lean, 40
part of new process, 12
of skills, 38–39
of work in progress, 39
managers, role of, 33, 37–40
material/environmental waste, as
type of waste, 14
micromanagement, 29
momentum, ix, xi, 34, 76
mono-skilled Super7s, 72
motion (of people), as type of
waste, 7, 14
muda (waste), 23
multi-skilled personnel, 24, 25
multi-skilled Super7 teams, 13, 72
mura (fluctuation), 23

N

Net Promoter Score (NPS), 11,
21, 47
non-quality, as type of waste, 14
non-safety, as type of waste, 14
norms, 29, 31, 38

O

objectives and goals

NOTES

NOTES

NOTES

NOTES

NOTES

NOTES

NOTES

_____

_____

_____

_____

_____

_____

_____

_____

_____

_____

_____

_____

_____

_____

_____

_____

_____

_____

_____

_____

_____